THE
NEW ENGLAND
PATRIOTS

Published by Creative Education, Inc., 123 South Broad Street, Mankato, Minnesota 56001

Library of Congress Catalog Card No.: 85-72621

ISBN: 0-88682-039-1

THE
NEW ENGLAND
PATRIOTS

JAMES R. ROTHAUS

CREATIVE EDUCATION

Babe Parilli hands off to powerful fullback Jim Nance. Nance set an AFL rushing record in '66 — 1,458 yards!

A TEAM GROWS
IN BOSTON

The people of Boston, Massachusetts, like to build things. When settlers built their first log cabins here in 1630, Boston was no more than a rocky little chunk of land almost totally surrounded by water.

Today, more than 350 years later, Boston looks a lot different. Entire hills have been moved, swamp lands have been made into thriving business centers, and the city is now adorned by spectacular, man-made landscape. Yes, the people of Boston sure like to build things.

For many years, Boston, the home of baseball's Red Sox, basketball's Celtics and hockey's Bruins, tried to build itself a professional football team, too. In the 1930's, the Redskins of the National Football League played in Boston before moving to Washington, D.C.; they're still in our nation's capital today.

Another team, called the Boston Yanks, kept football fans here happy until it, too, left town. More than a half-dozen teams tried to survive in New England. None of them made it.

It was easy to be discouraged, but remember, the Bostonians had built their own city—and a few disappointing setbacks weren't about to stop them from having their own football team.

One man in particular wanted such a team in Boston. His name was William H. Sullivan, but everyone called him Billy.

Did you know?

In the years leading up to Billy Sullivan's final successful launching of the Patriots, more than a half-dozen professional teams had failed to make the grade in New England.

Billy Sullivan had worked his way to the top of a major oil company, but pro football was his true love. In 1959, when a new league began to compete with the old, established NFL, Sullivan jumped at the chance to bring one more team to Boston. He just knew his team would succeed, where others hadn't. Sullivan's life-long motto was, "The best is yet to come." And so Boston was awarded the eighth and final franchise in the new American Football League.

THE BUILD-UP BEGINS

Now, Sullivan really had to start building. First he lured Mike Holovak away from his position as head football coach at Boston College, to become director of player personnel. Next, Billy went all the way to Western Illinois University to sign Lou Saban as the team's first head coach.

A local newspaper held a contest to name the team, and 74 different people came up with the winning choice: "Patriots." Everything was set—except for one little problem. Where would the Patriots play?

There were several possible locations: Fenway Park, Boston College and Harvard University were the top choices. But none was available. Sullivan finally settled on Boston University's field. Over the next 10 years, the Patriots would play on five different fields before finding a permanent home.

The Patriots, or "Pats" as fans began to call them, opened up their first training camp ever in the summer of 1960. More than 350 players showed up with dreams

Linebacker Nick Buoniconti (85) was among the NFL's most feared defenders of the 60's.

of playing pro ball. Some were second- and third-string former college players … others were All-Americans with an impressive reputation to live up to.

There was Ed "Butch" Songin. He had been a star quarterback at Boston College many years earlier, even though football wasn't even his best sport! Songin was considered the best American-born collegiate hockey player ever. But an injury cut short his hockey career, so he switched to football. He signed with the Cleveland Browns of the NFL, but was again injured and then cut. Songin played a couple of seasons in the Canadian Football League before deciding to return to his hometown of Walpole, Massachusetts.

Ed was 36 years old, working as a parole officer and playing semipro football for $50 a game when he joined the Pats. In his first game, an exhibition against Buffalo, Songin looked different from the other players—he was wearing his old hockey pads to protect his shoulders, instead of standard football gear! Still, Ed went out and completed 20 of 48 passes and threw for two touchdowns to lead Boston to a 28-7 victory in the AFL's first game ever.

Another "no-name" player in 1960 was a skinny fullback by the name of Larry Garron. He had played under Coach Saban in college, but at 165 pounds, Garron was too small to play pro ball—or so everyone thought.

Saban knew Garron had a special quality about him. Once, in a championship game at Wester, Illinois, Garron insisted on playing with a broken shoulder—and he scored three touchdowns!

The rest of the Patriots didn't know all this, of course. All they saw was a puny "coach's favorite" who kept

Jim Plunkett lit a fire under the '71 Patriots — and was named AFC Rookie of the Year in the bargain.

fumbling the ball or dropping passes.

"Garron is the first man alive to have thumbs in the middle of his palms," they laughed. Finally, Saban released him. But Garron didn't give up. He knew what he had to do. He joined the Boston YMCA and started lifting weights. While his teammates were playing games that first season, he was fervently pumping iron in that dim, lonely room. The hard work paid off.

By training camp of the next year, Garron weighed in at a rock-solid 195 pounds—still scrawny for a pro fullback—but his unfailing courage and quickness made up for it. He started in 1961 and, though a broken ankle benched him nine games into the season, the Pats knew he was there to stay.

And finally, perhaps the biggest surprise from among those 350 players who tried out at the 1960 training camp was Gino Cappelletti. Coach Saban had flown to Minnesota to meet with a prospective halfback named Bobby Cox. At their meeting, Cox introduced his friend, Cappelletti.

Cappelletti had played at Minnesota five years earlier and had tryouts both with the NFL and Canadian Football League teams, but the best he'd ever really done was being named All-Army quarterback when he served with the U.S. armed forces. When he met Saban, Cappelletti was working in a saloon in Minneapolis, making $80 a week, and playing in a touch football league twice a week.

Needless to say, Saban wasn't too impressed. He pretty much forgot about Cappelletti until the persistent Gino called to ask for a tryout. It took Saban two weeks to call back. When he did, he said, with a long-distance

Randy Vataha pulls in another Plunkett pass. The two friends seemed electronically wired on the field.

shrug, "Well, I guess you've got as good a chance to make this team as anybody."

Cappelletti—whose nickname was "the Duke"—knew he didn't have a good enough arm to be a pro quarterback. He was a good kicker, but teams in those days didn't carry kicking specialists. So Cappelletti told Saban he was a defensive back.

"I had played a little defense in college," he explained later, "and I'd always had the knack of being around the ball. Also, I wasn't afraid to hit. I knew every coach likes hitters, and if I threw my body around, I had a chance of lasting at least until they started looking for kickers."

Fortunately for the Patriots, that's just what happened.

Midway through Boston's first season, Cappelletti discovered in practice that he could catch the ball, too. And in the last game of 1960, the player who began the season starting at defensive back, finished it at receiver.

Ten years later, Gino Cappelletti and his number 20 jersey were retired by the Patriots. The Duke is still the team's career scoring leader, with a whopping 1,130 points, almost double the total of second-place scorer, kicker John Smith.

THE FIRST SEASONS LOOK GOOD

That first season, 1960, the Pats won five games and lost nine. The next year Boston traded with Oakland for veteran quarterback Babe Parilli. But many of the Patriot's draft choices, who also had been chosen in the NFL draft, signed with the rival league. Still, with Parilli,

Songin, Garron and Cappelletti, Boston's team remained powerful. Over the next four seasons, the Patriots won 35 games, lost just 17, and tied four.

At the start of the 1961 season, however, the team was down, and so were the fans. Boston was 2-3 when Billy Sullivan fired Lou Saban and promoted Mike Hovolak to head coach.

The players couldn't have been happier. Hovolak had always been the one assistant they could go to with their troubles. He was a father figure, and he stuck with his boys through good times and bad. The players appreciated his loyalty to them, and they rewarded him with winning seasons.

During those four great years, Boston had records of 9-4-1, 9-4-1, 7-6-1 and 10-3-1. Oddly enough, it was the 7-6-1 season—1963—that took the Patriots to the AFL Championship game.

After the season-opening game in 1961 was played at Boston College Stadium, the Pats had moved into Fenway Park, where they'd stay for six years. Now more fans could watch Babe Parilli and two second-year players lead their team to the '63 title game.

Linebacker Nick Buoniconti was just 5-11 and 220 pounds; what he lacked in size, however, he made up in speed, brains and hitting power. Meanwhile, offensive lineman Billy Neighbors opened up gigantic holes for Patriot backs. At the end of the 1963 regular season, Boston and Buffalo were tied for first place in their division.

The playoff game was set for December 28 in Buffalo. To Boston's dismay, a huge snowstorm hit just before the game; surely the Bills, who were used to such playing conditions, would walk right over the Pats. To make matters worse, Lou Saban now coached Buffalo, and he had a few bones to pick with his former employers.

The field was frozen solid. Both teams wore sneakers (instead of cleats) for better traction. But the Patriots refused to be distracted by the weather—their one aim was to win this game, and win they did. Garron scored 12 points on two touchdowns, and Cappelletti, who had to keep changing his right sneaker for a square-toed kicking shoe, booted four field goals and two extra points. The final score was 26-8. The Patriots were in the championship game!

The weather in San Diego, where Boston was to meet the Chargers, was about as different from Buffalo's weather as it could be. The dry, 70-degree heat wearied the Patriots early, and San Diego's Keith Lincoln took advantage.

Lincoln, the handsome young fullback, could do no wrong. He ran the ball 13 times for 206 yards and one touchdown. He caught seven more passes for 123 yards and another TD. He even completed his only pass attempt for 20 yards. When the final gun sounded, Lincoln's Chargers were AFL champs by a score of 51-10. Back to the drawing board for the Patriots.

THE VETERANS
GROW OLD

It wasn't exactly like lightning striking. No tornado touched down, and there was no volcanic eruption. No, when the Patriots' record dropped from 10-3-1 in 1964

They said it couldn't be done. At 5'5", "Mini Mack" Herron was supposed to be "too small" to make the NFL. He started from 1973-75.

The "Hog." Big John Hannah came to the team in 1973, and was still going strong in '85. He is easily one of the best offensive linemen in NFL history.

to 4-8-2 the very next year, a natural disaster wasn't at fault. It was the simple passing of time. Boston's players were getting old.

Coach Holovak's loyalty to his players worked two ways. He stood by them through thick and thin, and they, in return, gave him all they had. When age and injuries began to take their toll on the Boston team, Holovak just couldn't bear to cut his old friends. So for 11 years, from 1965 through 1975, the weary Patriots had only one winning season, nine losing campaigns, and one with equal numbers of wins and losses. The total read 49 wins, 98 losses and five ties.

Sure, these were tough times for the Patriots and their fans. Even so, there were plenty of golden moments along the way. Perhaps the most memorable of all were turned in by a giant running back named Jim Nance.

Jim Nance played his college ball at Syracuse, where great runners seemed to spring spontaneously from the earth each spring. Nance himself was a pretty good running back in college, but he felt as if his best efforts had always been overshadowed by the great Syracuse superstars of the past. This made Nance unhappy; and when he wasn't happy, he ate.

The Patriots drafted Nance in the ninth round of the 1965 college draft. When he walked into camp that summer, however, the Boston coaches knew immediately why their fullback was nicknamed "Big Bo." He had ballooned to 260 pounds!

Nance, a former NCAA wrestling champion, was still fast for his size, and Holovak wanted to give him a fair chance at running back. But finally, after weeks of so-so practice by Nance, the Boston coach took Big Bo aside

Did you know?

Patriots field-goal kicker Tony Franklin was credited with the second-longest field goal in NFL history—a 59-yarder at Dallas during his rookie campaign. By the way, Tony kicks barefooted!

Did you know?

Big John Hannah, the Patriots' handsome offensive tackle, has been called one of the top-five linemen ever to play the game. John's nickname? His teammates affectionately call him, "The Hog."

and gave him a choice.

"You block pretty well," Holovak said. "How would you like to be switched to guard? If you don't get your weight down in a hurry, next week you start working out with the linemen."

That did it. Nance lost 14 pounds in one week and left the bench to regain his position at starting fullback. The next season, he showed up for camp weighing 235, and that year, he ran over, through and—though rarely—around AFL defenses for a league record 1,458 yards.

Nance once revealed two of his secrets: First, he used his love of food for motivation before a big game. His last meal would be 16 hours before the kickoff. "Hunger makes me mad," Big Bo said, and by game time his disposition matched his growling stomach.

Bo's other secret reveals why he became one of the most-feared running backs in the game. "I've been noticing," he observed one day, "that when a guy hits me head-on, he's not quite so quick to hit me the next time. So I keep running at him, and pretty soon he starts to turn his shoulder. Then I know I've got him. When a man turns his shoulder on me, I'm going to get past him before he turns back."

That second year of Nance's pro career turned out to be Boston's only winning season in a decade. Problems continued with coaches and facilities: Clive Rush replaced Holovak in 1969; John Mazur took the head coaching title in 1970. The Pats' home field returned to Boston College in 1969, where in one game, the wooden bleachers caught fire and almost burned down. The Patriots played at Harvard in 1970, the year the two rival football leagues merged. Thereafter, the club would play in

The "fireman." Don Calhoun (44) always came to the rescue when the offense needed help.

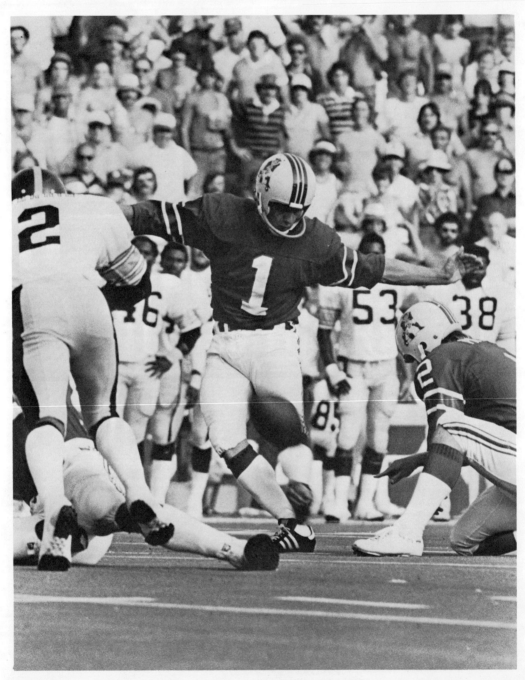

Kicker John Smith led the league in scoring with 115 points in 1979.

the Eastern Division of the NFL's American Football Conference.

The outlook took a turn for the better in 1971. First, Schaefer Stadium opened in Foxboro, Massachusetts. The new location prompted the team to change its name to the New England Patriots, thereby attracting more fans from beyond the Boston area. And second, the Pats came out of the 1971 draft with an exciting, 6-3, 220-pound quarterback named Jim Plunkett.

PLUNKETT
LIGHTS A FIRE

Plunkett, who won the Heisman Trophy as a senior at Stanford University, was smart, tough and physically gifted. He also had a magic sense for doing the right thing at the right time, whether on the field or off.

For example, Plunkett could have turned pro one year earlier because he had red-shirted one season at Stanford. But the dark-haired signal-caller with that burning glow in his eyes chose to stay at Stanford one more year, risking a possible poor season or, even worse, a career-ending injury. His reason? He felt he owed it to the school, the coaches and his teammates. That's the kind of leader Jim Plunkett was.

It didn't take long for this untested rookie to find his niche with the Patriots. Plunkett beat out veteran QB Mike Taliaferro to start for the season opener, and he stayed on the field for every offensive play the rest of the year.

Plunkett had a hand in the Patriots' fortunes off the

field, too. He suggested that head coach John Mazur give a tryout to one of Plunkett's old college teammates, Randy Vataha.

You couldn't help but like Randy Vataha. He was friendly and outgoing, and his tousled hair and quick smile kept everyone around him relaxed and happy. But Mazur had his doubts about Vataha's future as a pro receiver—after all, Randy was only 5-11. Vataha was so slightly-built that one summer he spent his college vacation playing the role of Bashful, one of the Seven Dwarfs, at Disneyland.

But Vataha was very quick. Perhaps more importantly, he knew when and where his buddy Plunkett liked to throw the ball. The two fit together like matching pieces in a puzzle. And, for one special game in 1971, the entire New England team fit together, too.

The Patriots had lost to Miami once already that season, a 41-7 whipping under the sweltering Florida sun. They had won four and lost seven games in all, and now they were to host the Dolphins in Schaefer Stadium.

Patriot fans looked sadly at each other and shook their heads when Miami's Mercury Morris caught the opening kickoff and weaved 94 yards for a touchdown. But Plunkett didn't even blink. He trotted onto the field, knowing full well that in the previous 11 games he had called running plays to open the game. Not this time. His first seven calls were all for passes, and he completed every one of them. The eighth play was a run, and big Jim Nance churned his gigantic legs right through Miami's famed defense and into the end zone for six points.

The next kickoff was also a disaster—but this time

From 1967-77, speed merchant Ike Forte (38) terrorized enemy defenses.

for the Dolphins. They fumbled. On the next play, Plunkett took the snap, dropped back, and watched Vataha fly by Miami cornerback Tim Foley. Vataha wasn't "bashful" on this play—he wriggled his way past the backpedaling Foley and caught Plunkett's perfect toss for another TD. Two field goals for New England and one for Miami made the half-time score, 20-10.

The Dolphins pulled to within seven points on another field goal in the third quarter. Then, it was Plunkett's turn again. He spotted Vataha darting over the middle and spiraled the ball right to his numbers; the play gained 38 yards to the Miami 25.

The rookie quarterback knew Miami wouldn't be expecting another pass to Vataha right away, so that's exactly what he called. Randy was wide-open in the end zone, and now the score was 27-14. Before time expired, New England defender Larry Carwell even got into the act with a 53-yard interception return for a touchdown. The final score was 34-14.

Vataha got the game ball, and Plunkett later was named AFC Offensive Rookie of the Year. But after the game, when the pair came out on the field for a television interview, a strange chant rose from the crowd. The 61,000 fans who had turned out for the game had just learned that the previous day was Vataha's 23rd birthday, and that day, Plunkett turned 24. What else could the crowd do? They sang "Happy Birthday" to their two young heroes, of course!

| **Did you know?** |

The son of a former Samoan boxing champ, fullback Mosi Tatupu spends the off-season in San Diego where he is active in community affairs and in running a shaved ice store called, "The Snowin' Samoan's Hawaiian Style Shaved Ice Store!"

When the Patriots went 10-6 in 1980, Mike Patrick was thinking Super Bowl. But it was not to be.

Life only got harder for the Patriots in 1972. An inexperienced offensive line let too many defenders put Plunkett on his back. Gradually, a string of minor injuries slowed him down.

Meanwhile, the front office was having its own troubles. Coach Mazur resigned, general manager Upton Bell was fired and Phil Bengston took over as coach for the tail-end of a dismal 3-11 season.

New England's record may not have looked much better over the next three years, but some good things were definitely happening to the team.

In 1973, Chuck Fairbanks, the successful coach at the University of Oklahoma, came to coach the Patriots. That year, the Pats acquired some great rookies, such as offensive guard John Hannah, fullback Sam Cunningham and wide receiver Darryl Stingley. They also signed little 5-foot-5 "Mini-Mack" Herron from the Canadian Football League, and gigantic offensive lineman Leon Gray.

The team went 5-9 that year (1973), but the individual talent meshed into a single team during the '74 training camp. Fairbanks installed a 3-4 defense, with three down linemen and four linebackers, and the team exploded to a 6-1 start in '74 before running out of gas and finishing the season at 7-7.

Plunkett's injuries lingered and worsened. Finally, the Patriots turned to another big quarterback, rookie Steve Grogan out of Kansas State. Grogan filled in admirably, although the team's record fell to 3-11.

Now the Patriots had two quarterbacks, and Plunkett wasn't happy. He was traded to San Francisco for back-up Tom Owen and four draft choices.

Fairbanks' plan finally fell into place in 1976. He drafted two defensive backs, Mike Haynes and Tim Fox, who started immediately in the Pats' secondary. Second-year players Russ Francis at tight end and Rod Shoate at linebacker improved with every game.

And so did Grogan. No, he was not another Plunkett. He didn't have a cannon for an arm. But, unlike Plunkett, he could run the ball as well as any player on the team. Fairbanks encouraged him to run, putting more pressure on the opposing defenses.

Give credit to the rest of the Patriots. too. Versatile running back Andy Johnson was as adept at catching the ball as he was at carrying it. Burly fullback Sam "Bam" Cunningham bulldozed enemy defenders; his back-up, Don Calhoun, finessed them. The deep threat, of course, was provided by high-flying receiver Darryl Stingley.

Together at last, the Pats could do no wrong. They won their last six games.

Though their opponent in the first round of the AFC playoffs was the big, bad Oakland Raiders, the New England players were understandably confident. After all, they had defeated the Raiders in an earlier regular-season game by a whopping 31 points, 48-17. And, sure enough, going into the final quarter, the Pats were on top, 21-10.

Then Ken "The Snake" Stabler took over. The crafty southpaw QB mustered every ounce of his experience to pick apart the Patriots' defense. With 11 minutes to

Young Steve Grogan, who liked to call his own plays in 1979, became the trigger man in one of the NFL's best passing attacks. Grogan was still with the team 6 years later.

go, Mark Van Eeghan bulled over the left side of the line for a Raiders touchdown, slashing the Pats' lead to just 21-17.

New England couldn't move the ball on either of its next two possessions. Oakland's defense was playing super-tough, and 56,000 screaming Raider fans rallied them on. Stabler got the ball back with 4:12 to go.

The Snake's laser-sharp passes carved away at the New England secondary. With 84 seconds remaining, Stabler took the snap at the Patriots 19. New England's young defensive line surged forward, and Mel Lunsford caught Stabler for an eight-yard loss. Now, it was third-and-18 at the 27-yard-line, with only 57 seconds to go. Could the Patriots hold on?

Stabler dropped back, and again the defensive rush was on. This time, nose guard Ray Hamilton got to Kenny just as he released the ball. It fell incomplete. But Hamilton's follow-through with his hand made contact with Stabler's head. Tweeet! Roughing the passer was the official's call, and even Hamilton later admitted it was a proper one.

So it was first down at the 13, and it was here that the Patriots lost their poise. Another flag fell, this time for unsportsmanlike conduct. Two plays later, Stabler rolled out to his left, saw an opening and dived the last yard over the goal line. The extra point was good, and Oakland stayed alive in the playoffs with a 24-21 win.

When the Raiders won the Super Bowl a few weeks later, all the Patriots could do was shake their heads and think about what might have been.

31

THE YEAR OF THE SIT-OUT

"The Year of the Sit-out." That's how many Patriot fans remember 1977. Two players, offensive linemen John Hannah and Leon Gray, refused to practice or play until their salaries were increased. Before they returned and played their way back into shape, New England had lost twice. The Pats went on to win eight of their last 11 games to finish 9-5, but five losses were enough to keep them out of the playoffs.

The following season—1978—dawned with the experts picking the Pats to go all the way. New England had picked up two more starters in the draft—wide receiver Stanley Morgan and defensive back Raymond Clayborn. With those additions, the Patriots boasted one of the deepest talent pools in the league. The young draftees from earlier years were now entering the prime of their careers. One veteran in particular, Darryl Stingley, felt confident he was approaching his peak.

THE COURAGE OF DARRYL STINGLEY

Darryl Stingley grew up in Chicago, where he acquired that certain "street sense" that only inner-city kids seem to have. But young Stingley had several other qualities that would eventually make him a truly special professional athlete.

An honor student in high school, Stingley always had a smile for a friend or teammate. On the football field

Towering (6'6", 242 pounds) Russ Francis, a sticky-fingered end who could catch the impossible, later jumped ship to the San Francisco 49ers.

Little Stanley Morgan roared into the 1984 season as the Patriots' all-time leading pass reception leader.

he developed a reputation as a fearless receiver. With the approaching footsteps of angry would-be tacklers closing in on him, Darryl would still leap high in the air for the catch. Darryl took that courage into an exhibition game with the Oakland Raiders in 1978, never suspecting that he would have to be carried on a stretcher from the field.

It happened so quickly. Grogan dropped back as Stingley sprinted five yards downfield and then slanted across the turf diagonally. Grogan released the ball . . . it sailed slightly high. Stingley, eyes intently focused on the ball, coiled and leaped high into the air. Oakland defensive back Jack Tatum timed his hit to contact Stingley's outstretched body in mid-air. The impact was a horrible thing to behold. Seconds later, Stingley lay perfectly still on the field. He wasn't moaning, or holding an injured joint, or rolling over. Just—motionless.

Doctors rushed onto the field. They fitted a collar around Stingley's neck to keep his head still. One reached into his bag and pulled out a rubber mallet to test Darryl's reflexes, but there was no response. The ambulance sped him to a nearby hospital where X-rays confirmed the worst fears: Darryl Stingley's neck had been snapped and broken. Like a rag doll, the courageous athlete lay paralyzed from the neck down.

Back on the field, his teammates had no way of knowing how badly Darryl had been hurt, and they went on to defeat the Raiders, 21-7. It was in the dressing room that Coach Fairbanks broke the news.

"Men, I'd like to tell you about Darryl," he began, but his voice trailed off and they knew at once that Stingley would never play again. There in the locker room, the

Patriots wept and prayed together for their friend.

Stingley stayed in the California hospital, with his wife by his bedside. Several times related problems, such as pneumonia, put Darryl's life on the line. The same enduring courage he had always shown on the field now pulled him through the toughest match-up he had ever faced.

While Stingley was fighting for his life, his teammates were dedicating their season to him. Messages were sent back and forth. Stingley and his teammates kept their ties. When the Patriots returned to Oakland for their regular-season meeting, Billy Sullivan visited Stingley in his hospital room before the game.

"Is there anything we can do for you, Darryl?" the New England owner asked.

"Just one thing, Mr. Sullivan," came Stingley's reply. "Beat Oakland."

The Pats did just that, of course—for Darryl. In all, New England won 11 of 16 games in 1978 and finished first in the AFC East, only to lose to Houston and its new super rookie, Earl Campbell, 31-14, in the playoffs.

It appeared from the outside just a few weeks earlier that everything was going New England's way, but all was not well. Fairbanks had been approached by officials from the University of Colorado. They wanted him to leave the Patriots and move to Boulder, and they were willing to pay top dollar for him to return to college coaching.

The Pats had one final regular-season game—plus the playoffs—still to go. But Billy Sullivan just couldn't let his team be coached by a man whose heart was somewhere else. He told Fairbanks to stop talking to

Iron man! For more than a decade, rangy linebacker Steve Nelson was the driving force of the Patriots' defense. (1984)

Colorado until the Pats either won the Super Bowl or were eliminated from the playoffs. When Fairbanks refused, Sullivan suspended him, and the Pats lost to Miami in the final regular-season game.

Fairbanks returned to coach the Pats in the Houston game, but the damage had already been done. The Patriots, whose chances for Super Bowl rings had been the best in club history, closed the season on a disappointing note.

All in all, 1978 had been a bittersweet year for the Patriots. Their tremendous talent and desire were not enough to offset the distracting front-office problems, and Stingley's tragic injury still hung like a cloud over the entire camp.

Optimists were convinced that the Patriots could put together the pieces again for another run at the Super Bowl in 1979. But it was not meant to be. They finished second in the AFC East at 9-7. Their record improved to 10-6 in 1980, but again New England just missed the playoffs.

Following Fairbanks' departure to Colorado, assistant coach Ron Erhardt took the reins. Erhardt worked feverishly to put the Patriots back into championship contention. He worked overtime with the younger players, traded for proven veterans and revamped both the offense and defense. But the harder he tried, the more disappointing the results. In 1981, the Pats hit rock bottom. They finished last in the division with a 2-14 mark.

It wasn't entirely Erhardt's fault. Grogan had injured his neck early in the season. When he returned to the line-up, his knee gave out. Young Matt Cavanaugh took over, but with little success. Only the running of Vagas Ferguson, Tony Collins and Cunningham, who broke Nance's team rushing record, kept the club from falling further.

Erhardt threw up his hands after the Pats' final loss of the year at Baltimore. "I've done all I can with this team," he said. Sullivan agreed. Three weeks later, he named Ron Meyer, formerly with Southern Methodist University, as the new head coach.

A NEW GENERATION OF PATRIOTS

Meyer took a look around the New England training room and came to an important conclusion. "There are two ways to improve your team," he said. "You can do it with youth or experience. I think young players, with help from selected veterans, are the answer here."

On draft day, Meyer put his youth movement into operation, swapping starters Russ Francis, Rod Shoate and Tim Fox for draft picks. In the draft, Meyer selected Ken Sims of Texas and Andre Tippett of Iowa to shore up a creaky defense. Both players eventually moved into the starting line-up and, together with linebacker Steve Nelson and long-standing vet Julius Adams, the Pats now had a powerful pass rush. Offensively, Meyer went for line help, taking Darryl Haley, a tackle from Utah. Now Grogan would have more time to throw the ball.

It didn't take long for Meyer's youth brigade to make a difference. Following a nine-week players' strike, the

Pats stormed through their remaining games, winning three of their last four. Two of those wins were shutouts. It had been two years since New England had held an opponent scoreless; now they had two in consecutive weeks!

Grogan was leading a better-balanced offense, throwing long to Morgan and pitching wide to Collins for his patented sideline sprints. It all added up to a 5-4 record and a berth in the playoffs for the first time since 1978. There, however, the Pats' inexperience showed as they fell to Miami, 28-13.

Meyer said he was pleased with the improvement, but his job was only half-done. "Now it's time to overhaul the offense," he said. "There's always room for more game-breakers there."

It was no secret that Grogan, who had doubled as a passer and runner for eight seasons, was in need of relief help. Meyer, hoping to add more passing punch to the quarterback position, drafted the pride of Illinois— "Champagne" Tony Eason—to fill the bill.

Eason had rewritten nearly all the Big Ten passing marks with the Illini. The Patriots, who hadn't had a game-breaking quarterback since the days of Plunkett, hoped he would do more of the same as a pro.

Eason and several other rookies got more game time than they expected in 1983, but for all the wrong reasons. The Patriots were hit hard by injuries. Grogan broke his leg late in the season. Center Peter Brock blew his knee out. In the final four weeks of the year, it would be up to "Champagne" Tony to put the fizz back in the New England offense. Unfortunately, Eason and the Pats fell short, going 2-2 and just missing the playoffs.

The one-and-only John Hannah leads a quarterback raiding party in 1984.

Here's why Patriots rushing leader Tony Collins made the Pro Bowl in only his third year in the league. (1984)

Meyer wasn't disappointed in Eason's showing. In fact, he now wanted to build the Pats' game around Champagne's strong arm. New England's offense, which was geared to the run, had to become more explosive and score more points.

Fortunately, in the 1984 draft the Patriots had the first pick overall, so they chose Nebraska wide receiver Irving Fryar, a sure-handed speed merchant. Now, Meyer had two outstanding receivers in Morgan and Fryar, but he still wanted to make room for one more—tight end Derrick Ramsey. To do that, the coach dropped a running back and added a third receiver, Ramsey. Collins, Mosi Tatupu and Craig James would now alternate in the one-back formation.

The New England press openly questioned Meyer's tactics. After all, New England had been one of the NFL's great running teams. After the Pats lost to Miami twice in the first half of the 1984 season, Sullivan yielded to the critics. He fired Meyer and hired Raymond Berry as his replacement.

THE BEST
IS YET TO COME

Raymond Berry? The same Raymond Berry who had terrorized the league as a superstar pass receiver for the Colts several years before? The same guy who had quietly worked behind the scenes as an assistant coach with the Pats to transform Stanley Morgan, Darryl Stingley and Russ Francis into Pro Bowl standouts? Yup, the very same guy.

Did you know?

Let's hear it for the old guy! Defensive end Julius "The Jewel" Adams entered the 1984 season as the NFL's oldest (36) active defensive lineman—and still one of the best.

Now the whole team would become Berry's responsibility. He faced an uphill task in taking the job at midseason. New England, at 5-3, needed to win all remaining games to qualify for the '84 playoffs. Though they ultimately managed only four more victories to finish 9-7, the campaign marked a new beginning for the Patriots.

For one thing, Eason stole the quarterback slot from Grogan. It happened in an '84 game against the hard-hitting Seattle Seahawks. With the 'Hawks leading, 23-0, in the second quarter, Eason came in to spell Grogan for awhile. Surprise! Eason not only rallied the team, the Pats went on to ring up 38 unanswered points to win the game.

Eason hung in there the rest of the season to establish himself as one of the NFL's brightest young stars, finishing third in league passing by hitting on 23 touchdown passes.

Heading into the second half of the 1980's, Eason had the best back-up QB in the league in Grogan. He had an outstanding array of moving targets in Morgan, Fryar, Ramsey and Stephen Starring. Wait, there's more. The Patriots offensive line was still anchored by the one-and-only John Hannah. And, should an occasional drive get stalled, the Pats could still call on deadly bare-foot placekicker Tony Franklin for the automatic 3-pointer.

On defense, the Patriots' talent pool seemed to just go on and on, deeper and deeper. Among others, the Patriots' stop-squad featured hardnosed guys like Nelson, Tippett, Clayborn and safety Roland James.

It all adds up to a string of inevitable playoff appear-

Cornerback Ray Clayborn hauls in another juicy interception in 1984. The previous year, Ray batted down 22 enemy passes!

Fearsome linebacker Andre Tippett promised "quarterbacks for breakfast" at the onset of the 1985 campaign.

ances in the years to come … and, at least on paper, there should be a Super Bowl real soon for the New England fans. Now that would be the most exciting thing to happen in Massachusetts since the American Revolution.

Even now, on a breezy autumn day, you can hear the fans chanting, "The Patriots are coming! The Patriots are coming!" Indeed, the best is yet to come.